Cover **Edgar Gonzales**

PERSONAL SECURITY MANUAL

TERRORISM: THE NEW WAR
Guidelines and Procedures
AGAINST: KIDNAPPINGS
TERRORIST ATTACKS, THEFTS, AND
NATURAL DISASTERS

PERSONAL SECURITY MANUAL
Guidelines and Procedures

PERSONAL SECURITY MANUAL
Guidelines and Procedures

My. PN P. (r) Edgar Gonzales

INDEX

TELEPHONE PROTECTION
Introduction, Useful Information for Terrorists and Criminals, Data Extraction, Answering Procedures, Auxiliary Telephone Systems

PHONE THREATS
Types of Calls, Never Ignore Calls But Always Act as Expected, Emergency Procedures, Receiving Phone Threat, Procedures After the Call, Telephone Threat Information

IDENTIFICATION AND HANDLING OF MAIL AND PACKAGES THAT MAY HAVE BOMBS
Explosive Letters, Actions with Suspicious Mail, Explosive Packages, Marking the Mail Examined by X-rays or Metal Detector

HOSTAGE SURVIVAL
Hostage Preparation, The Kidnap, Imprisonment, Post-trauma Behavior, Against the Kidnappers

CHAPTER III

PERSONAL SECURITY PROCEDURES

PROCEDURES TO ADOPT IN CASE OF RECEIVING CORRESPONDENCE
Outside Appearance, Weight, Stiffness, Thickness, Address, Handwriting, Stamps

PROCEDURES TO ADOPT IN CASE OF AN EXPLOSION OR FINDING OF AN EXPLOSIVE DEVICE
What Must Be Done, What Must Not Be Done, Information Given to the Chief of the Deactivation Squad

PROCEDURE WHEN FINDING YOURSELF AS A HOSTAGE

PROCEDURES TO FOLLOW WHEN RECEIVING BOMB THREATENING PHONE CALLS
Procedures, Format of Bomb Threat

PROCEDURES TO CONTROL OFFICE VISITORS

PROCEDURES AND NORMS FOR MOBILIZATIONS SECURITY
Vulnerability Aspects, Choosing the Vehicle, Drivers (chauffeurs), Driving or Riding in Attacked Vehicles

PROCEDURE FOR THE USE OF GUNS

ARMORED VEHICLES: The Armor, Accessories

CHAPTER IV

DISASTERS
Common Disasters, Types of Disasters: Natural and Artificial, State of Emergency

EARTHQUAKES
Modified Mercalli Scale, Ritcher Scale, Procedures for Earthquakes, Specific Actions, Evacuating and Escape Routes for Earthquakes

PREVENTION AND FIRE CONTROL
Fire, Basic Procedures to Fight Fire, Types of Fire, Fire Prevention, Fire Rescue, Precautions

FLOODS
Possible Damage, Actions to Take if Person is Drowning During or After a Flood

ELECTRIC STORMS
Precautions In the House, Outside, In the Water, Lightning Strikes, Concepts

INTRODUCTION

I put at the disposition of the community, businesses, business personnel, and, in particular, all of the professionals who have the responsibility to protect and to safeguard the physical integrity of the citizens; this manual. The content of the various themes have been compiled from speciality manuals and through twenty years as a foreign consultant with the Peruvian Police in the fight against subversion and terrorism in Peru.

The Manual contains up-to-date guidelines and procedures to minimize and/or dissuade the risk of being kidnapped or attacked. Experience has demonstrated that the most vulnerable time for any victim is the time that he or she spends moving or in transit from home to work, thus more emphasis has been given to the techniques related to moving and transporting. We must not forget that social, political, and religious aspects motivate the terrorists and delinquents, forming the terror and the hate.

More than 90% of kidnappings and terrorist attacks have occurred in the street, which makes us believe that this is the place of most danger if no precaution is adopted. I state that under no security form is 100% of protection obtained, especially if it is a military-style and/or terrorist attack.

All human risks have been covered in this Manual, from the attack of a terrorist to a natural disaster. The procedures and methods to be considered for each have been explained, one by one, in a language that is understandable and detailed. Each risk has been grouped with other similar risks to promote an effective functionality with a common reference, consultation, and the distinct guarding forces, creating a general interest theme.

With this publication, in which practice and critics will evaluate, I want to contribute something beneficial to the security of the citizens of this country. It is my hope that this material will not be merely an "adornment" on a library shelf, just one more volume printed, but it is my wish that it is utilized and put into practice; security is a problem that belongs to all of us.

The Author

CHAPTER I

GENERAL RECOMMENDATIONS AND GUIDELINES FOR PERSONAL PROTECTION

GENERALITIES

The recommendations for personal security are to minimize the risk of being kidnapped or being injured in a malicious way and must be adequate to the individual and/or the family. These recommendations must be adapted to one's own respective life styles.

Concerning the issues on personal security of an Executive and/or VIP, it is vital to determine, as accurate as possible, the risk degree that has to be faced according to his operational activities as for his personal life, covering as close as 24 hours a day, 7 days a week. We must keep in mind that terrorists and criminals, before they act, do a patient and detailed observation, which will guide their actions. So the security recommendations must be the result of an evaluation of the risk degree that affects the individual. It must include his domestic habits, business habits, and the physical security of his home, office, entertainment places, and means of transportation before we pretend to adopt the protection measures for the Executives and/or personalities.

There are, nevertheless, principles and basic rules that can be set and simple ways that can be suggested which would be of great value to minimize the risks. The special thing on every Personal Protection Plan is simplicity, without the interference on the way of life. It is much more probable that a simple and realistic plan is taken than a plan with complex and exaggerated procedures.

PRINCIPLES IN PERSONAL PROTECTION

The next four principles will be applied to every aspect of personal security and must be kept in mind at all times:

- Be aware and suspicious, curious and inquisitive

- Be methodical when applying the proceedings

- Never establish a routine

- Establish a secure communication system with the police and/or security chief, in case of an emergency.

HOUSE PROTECTION

KEYS:

- No unauthorized person is have access to keys

- There must be a minimal number of keys per lock; there must be a record of spare keys.

- If a key is lost, all locks must be changed

- Never keep the keys on "safe places", for example, under an unused drawer or under a carpet, or tied to a rope placed on the mailbox. The keys must be placed on a safe place or with oneself.

DOORS:

- There should not be windows on the outdoor doors, if windows are present, they must be reinforced and laminated.

- The door and frame must have a solid construction.

- Every hinge must be placed on the indoor side of the door.

- There must a "magic eye" and a lens for interior TV circuit.

- Two strong locks (Horizontal superior and inferior) and a chain must be placed and used.

- There must be an intercom; the inner receptor must not be near the main door, but in anotherroom that does not face the area where the exterior receptor is.

- The exterior doors must be locked at all times, be especially careful with the backdoor of it is the most frequently used.

- The locks must be reinforced with "sleep locks"

- All exterior doors must be placed to resist a forced entry

- The door must be connected to the intruder alarm (if there is one)

- All personal Ids must be removed from doors, gates, and mailboxes.

WINDOWS:

- All windows must have locks

- There must be curtains or blinds.

- The curtains must be closed at night

- Windows must be connected to the intruder alarm (if there is one)

- It would be ideal if the windows were reinforced with solid shutters.

TELEPHONE:

- Treat the telephone as a mean of communication.

- Do not call before hand to give information about travels or visits.

- Do not give away your phone number indiscriminately.

- Make sure your phone number is not listed.

- When answering, do not mention your phone number or your name.

- The family members must be instructed not to give details about the whereabouts of the members of the house.

- Keep the police number or similar emergency number nearby.

- Always identify the calling number for checking the authenticity if necessary.

- If there is any suspicious or odd call, call the police.

- Have a simple password for the family, for emergency use. (For example, if forced to talk only by phone)

SERVICES: If there are exterior installations (such as the electricity or central heating) make sure they are physically protected and cannot be disconnected from the outside.

LIGHTS:

There must be adequate lights to illuminate:

- The area around the main door and backdoor for proper visit identification.

- Any dark place that can serve as a hideout.

- The lights that illuminate the exterior of the home must be placed indoors.

EMERGENCY BOX:

You must have an emergency box on some place known by the entire family. The box must have:

- Flashlight and spare batteries

- A First Aid kit with:
  Bandages for bullet wounds.
  The family's blood list.
  Coins for pay phones and/or phone cards.
  A nearby police station and hospital's phone number list
  A useful phone number list (including trusted neighbors)

DOMESTIC PERSONNEL:

Consider the following pointers:

- Make sure they do not have criminal records

- Verify the references

- Be wary when talking near them.

- Restrict key access.

SERVICE AND MAINTENANCE PERSONS:

The next procedures must be done to check on service or maintenance people:

- Everyone must have an appointment. Unexpected visits must not be allowed

- Ask for the name of the service person before his arrival.

- At his arrival, check the name provided by the employer with the one written and the photo ID (in case there is one).

- Be with the personnel while he works.

- All deliveries must be checked before accepted. In case of suspicions, ask the messenger to open the packages himself.

- If the identify of a regular service person, such as mailman or milkman, changes, check

- with the employer for authorization

CHILDREN:

- All children must be aware of the phone security conditions.

- The children must know when and how to ask for help.

- The children must not open the door to strangers.

ANSWERING THE DOOR:

The following procedures must be adhered to when opening the door to an expected or unexpected visitor:

- Visitors must have an appointment.

- Close circuit Identify the visitor with the intercom of the "magic eye" (or the TV, CCTV).

- Look for nervousness.

- Verify the identity when appropriate.

- Do not talk at the door.

- At night, illuminate the visitor, but keep the indoor lights off.

UNKNOWN VISTIORS OR DRIFTERS:

- At any time, especially at night, be wary with unexpected door knocks; more if it is from someone asking for help. Do not allow anyone to use the phone, even if his reasons appear to be truthful.

- If there are drifters near the house, call the police or local security.

      ALARMS: At least two emergency devices, connected to an intruder alarm, must be installed. One device located on the front door and the other device located in the indoor place of refuge.

      REFUGE: In areas where the threat ratio is high, there must be an indoor refuge. The objective is to provide a safe place in the house where the family can stay at night or in an emergency.

The refuge must be prepared to stand a physical attack, for as long as it takes the police to arrive in response to an emergency call. It must have a safe means of communication in case of an emergency.

DOGS: Experience has shown that dogs are an aid for protection and have a strong deterrent effect on intruders.

POLICE COORDINATION: Coordination with the police is an advantage for as long as the existence of such relation is kept confidential and at an adequate level.

NEIGHBORS: Good neighbor relations are essential. Neighbors can assist on an emergency and can keep an "eye" on the house when it is empty.

VEHICULAR PROTECTION

CAR: The vehicle must be kept in perfect condition at all times, and must have regular maintenance. The car must be of a common make and model, and must have unobtrusive coloring and accessories. It would be advantageous to have two cars to interchange regularly. For varying the usage pattern, it might be a consideration to rent your vehicle. It is recommended having good rearview mirrors, locks on the gas tank, trunk, and hood.
Also, consider a tamper alarm installation with internal indicators.

THE GARAGE: It is recommended having a garage with metal lift doors that can be operated by remote control. The garage must be locked at all times. It is an advantage to get in the garage without leaving the car.

QUICK CHECK: It is important to check under the car and inside of it, checking for abnormal things. It is particularly important if the car is not attended for a long time, for example, during the night or when parked for shopping. If there were a threat, it would be necessary to check the car before using it.

ROUTE SELECTION: It is of vital importance to think over carefully on the different routes to take to establish a known route. You must know the address of the police stations near the route to be used. Try to choose routes that do not have many traffic lights, or branching outs.

CHAUFFEUR: The use of a chauffeur (for example the wife) would be of great help for protection. The drop off and pick up places can be changed easily as well as the times to do so. This makes it is easier to watch from the car to see if it is surveyed or if there is some abnormal or suspicious activity.

PARKING: Use any authorized parking lot, but not always the same one.

CAR DOORS: On a moving car, all doors must be locked as well as the windows. These precautions must be taken as a standard discipline this rule will reduce the probabilities of kidnapping or breaking and entry on the car when it stops on certain places, such as traffic lights.

BUSES: If you have to take a bus, change the time and the bus stop used. The bus can also be taken as a way to vary the pattern for moving from one place to another. Nevertheless, there must be considered the disadvantages of it, such as getting exposed when waiting for it.

ON FOOT: Always avoid problem places; try to walk with the crowd and not alone. You must know the nearby police stations and do a mental check on the patrol cars in the neighborhood.

OFFICE PROTECTION

ENTRY CONTROL: There must be set an effective system to control the entry to the office complex so all people can be checked, as well as all briefcases, and which allows for verification of the identity of the visitors and escort them to the required offices.

OFFICE LOCATION: The office must be placed so that the visitor can gain entry only after he has passed the secretary's office.

OFFICE PROTECTION:

- All doors, except the secretary's office, must be locked at all time. Consider the possibility to install an emergency button in the secretary's office and in the executive's office.

- According to the offices' distribution plan; consider the possibility to install auxiliary security systems to restrict the access and to give protection against intruders and assaults. These could include the use of CCTV.

CONCLUSIONS

- A person is more vulnerable of kidnapping when arriving or leaving his home, office, or when moving from one place to another, therefore, avoid the routine on those activities and being aware of the risk minimizes the danger.

- Besides adhering to the principles written here, it is recommended to avoid as much as possible an activity regarding business, social or entertainment that could rise the probability of a kidnapping of any member of the family.

CHAPTER II

SECURITY RULES FOR PROTECTION

HOUSE PROTECTION

It is preferable, before selecting a place to live, to recognize the area to determine the following:

- **Physical Protection:** Is the place physically secure? (Generally speaking, an apartment is safer than a house)

- **Garage Protection:** Is there an inner door connecting the garage to the house? Is there a vulnerable place where the driver has to stop to open the gates that access the garage or the area?

- **Transport Protection:** Are the routes between the house and office acceptable according to general protection rules? There must be alternate paths adequate to drive fast or make evasive maneuvers.

- **Police and Arson:** Is there a police or fire station at an acceptable distance?

- **General Area:** Are the surrounding areas acceptable? It would be ideal live in a place inhabited by others like you, with the same lifestyles. If you were abroad, it would be beneficial that all countrymen live in one place.

PRECAUTIONARY MEASURES

- **Security Fence:** A solid fence must be built around the house. It should be dark and a minimum of 9.5 ft. (2.9m) high.

- **Clear Area:** Bushes and trees must be taken out in order to get a 100 ft (30m) clear area around the house. Grass is the best garden for safety. The area around the house must be orderly and clear to eliminate any intruder hideouts.

- **Entry Paths:** All access paths to the house must be checked. Entry paths must be minimal although it is necessary to keep other exits and entries as alternatives in case of fire. If it is necessary all doors and windows at an intruder's hand should be reinforced. Doors must be built solid and windows must have bars or shades if in an accessible place.

- **Lock:** As frequently as possible, curtains must be closed, shades and doors locked. This preferably at night.

- **Visitors Identification:** Outside doors must have "magic eyes" and chains. Never open them until visitors have been positively identified. (Even a police id must be verified by calling the station.)

- **Services:** All phone lines, power and gas must be verified to check if they are reasonably protected.

- **Alarm System:** An alarm operated by an intruder detector and manually operated for assault should be installed. It should have a siren, to alert the neighbors and deter the intruder. It would be ideal if it were connected to the police station or the security agency.

- **Exterior illumination:** There must be exterior illumination, with the light aimed at any intruder's eyes (lights can be turned on as the alarm system goes off).

- **Door Locks and Keys:** There must be security locks in all entries along the security fence and inside the residence. All locks must be changed when arriving to a new house or if the keys are lost.

- **Windows:** If the area is vulnerable to bombing, the glass of the windows should be exchanged with laminated glass or treated polyester adhesive to minimize injuries.

- **The Refuge:** The room in which a potential victim can get shelter in an emergency must be equipped as a "refuge". It must be of solid construction and have telephone and other means of communication with aid resources (by radio, megaphone, siren, or beacon light)

- **Front Gate:** In some situations, it is advisable to install an intercom between the front gate and the house (this can be combined with remote locks or bolts to control the gate from a distance.).

- **Dogs:** Dogs are a valuable aid for protection as well as for their inherent capacities as for their deterrent effect.

- **Name Protection:** The owner's name must not be placed on the gate, as well as not being placed in phone books or other records.

- **Workers:** All service men and visitors should be escorted when entering the residence area.

- **Deliveries:** Unidentifiable packages must never be accepted and precautions must be taken to check deliveries from vendors

- **Be Evasive:** A casual visitor should never have the chance to know whether the potential victim is in or out. For example, be prudent enough on the phone, always lock the doors of your garage, and make sure you cannot be seen from the outside while being in the yard or inside the house. When the house is to be left alone, keep a light on, and consider the possibility of installing automatic devices to turn the lights on and off.

- **Emergency Supplies:** You must store an adequate amount of supplies in case of an emergency. This must include canned food, drinkable water, candles, flashlights, portable stove, first aid kit, fire extinguisher and an axe. You should also consider an alternate power supply.

ALTERNATIVE LODGING

It would be of great value to get another house as an alternative, temporary living space. It must be a two-room apartment registered under another name. Its existence must be known only by a trusted person and must be recorded on the personal record so that its existence is known in case of an emergency (its existence should be placed on a sealed envelope). Such apartment can be useful to disappear for some days if there is temporary worry about the protection of your main residence or if the stress of living under constant protection turns unbearable for a moment. There must be taken all means to ensure the secrecy of the apartment or the potential danger will rise instead of reducing it.

THE REFUGE

The refuge's concept comes from the Norman's era, when part of a complex was reinforced or fortified to be used as sanctuary or as an additional security place when the exterior defences were overcome.

ALTERNATIVES

When an intruder tries to break in, the inhabitants have the chance to escape or stay on the place. The decision of escaping, although the most instinctive human reaction, has to be made as quickly as possible, n a crisis or when it is lest expected. A number of factors must be considered:

- The number of intruders

- From which direction they are coming

- If the place is surrounded

- Time to escape

- Other escape routes

- Select a route once you are out of the place

- Number of people to escape

- Location of the victims and time from attack

While escape plans offer a possible solution, they also tend to be more hazardous because you loose the cooperation of others involved in the initial plans. It is recommended having a refuge because it is simple. It requires minimum planning and it is safe. While assistance takes time, at least the rescue team knows where to find the victims.

DESIGN

Designing a refuge depends on the following:

- The number of people that will occupy the refuge

- Time to get there

- Time for the intruders to get there

- The design and structure of the place itself

Normally the refuge must be placed in a zone that provides a series of barriers before getting to the refuge itself; for example, doors, stairs, elevators, security personnel.

Ideally the refuge must have:

- **Solid walls, floors and roofs:** These must be bullet proof, but at least, it must prevent the entry until help arrives.

- **Doors:** The doors must be solid and normally bulletproof and with the ease of shutting and locking them quickly from inside. The methods usually preferred as coupling bolts and strings bolts. One should be able to look at the surrounding area through a magic eye on the door, for example.

- **Windows:** The refuge can have windows but these must be armored. They must have bars or steel blinds. The frames may also be reinforced.

COMMUNICATIONS

There must be devices installed to ensure communications: a radio (with spare batteries), a cellular phone or a phone with step proof lines. The radio antenna must be inside the refuge.

PROVISIONS

Depending on the refuge situation, the next supplies are recommended:

- Complete medical equipment

- Fire extinguishers that do not throw hazardous gases, carbon dioxide must not be released on closed or limited-area places.

- A fire blanket

- An electric fan for air circulation, a spare battery operated fan, in case the main one fails

- Emergency lights, fixed units, independent ones are preferable than a flashlight.

- Food supplies and cooking facilities, for example, a gas burner

- Recreation for children, including lots of paper and pencils

- An electric siren on top of the refuge or an air-compressed siren with an audible capacity of 110 dB (if recommended). The siren must point to the nearest trusted neighbor

- Neighbors must know about the siren and must be familiarized with its sound and must be aware of the conditions of the use of it.

- Water supply and water sterilization pills. The water must be replaced and be enough to allow water to flush the toilet.

- Toilet disinfectants.

PRACTICE:

It would be wise to practice, from time to time, the emergency procedures of moving into the refuge and locking it.

KEY USAGE SECURITY

Locks and keys are vital in the security system and protection of any industrial or commercial establishment. This element can be physically attacked, forced or picked. The security measures for keys are designed to protect against the threat that follows lost, theft, or key copying.

GENERAL PRINCIPLES

The ideal security system requires:
- All keys must be recorded and identified with a marking system, and a list of them has to be maintained.

- All work keys are placed on a central locker, shut with a combination lock and on a closed room and permanently watched.

- All spare keys have to be kept on a similar, but separated locker.

- Keys are delivered to named people who will sign a record and are to return them at the end of the day.

- All keys will be verified on the master record at the end of the working day

- The locks will be changed in case of missing of a key, even if a rapid search is done.

- A clear-written statement of the above.

These general principles are the only way for achieving an effective security system for keys, which in advance can be modified to meet all the principles listed.

IMPLEMENTATION PROGRAM

Identification: The first phase is to identify which keys are the most important. This will be achieved with a simple appreciation of those gates/doors that allow access to delicate areas than those that control movement in an area:

- Identify the internal priority areas.

- Identify the most important service installation.

- Identify who needs to carry keys and which type.

Record: This is the procedure to know the physical location of all the copies of the keys identified as most important:

- Locate all the copies of the important keys.

- In case doubt change the lock.

- Name a responsible that supervises the security system of keys.

- Get a security key-box with a combination lock.

- Set the box on an internal secure area.

- Establish a master record for all-important keys.

- Code with a number or color all the keys.

Control system: There is to be introduced an education and key verification system

- The key holder must sign a record for the key.

- It is to be immediately informed the loss of a key.

- Key-holders must not take the keys home.

- Keys that aren't kept on the box are to be regularly checked.

- Never less than 6 times a month.

- At least monthly in a high threat area.

High Security Areas: Consider the possibility of implementing a central storage and a strict daily check of keys corresponding to high security areas.

OFFICE SECURITY

OFFICICE LOCATION

If possible an office or plant must not be in a poor area or in a place where access is limited or through dangerous streets. To create an ideal circumstance, the next items should be considered:

- The facilities should be placed on its own land and should not be at other building site.

- The facilities must have its own perimeter, protected and well illuminated.

- A procedure must be taken to control access

- Parking must be inside the perimeter.

- The building must be well built with metal doors and frames especially on the first floor

- It should have two emergency exits from the building and the field

- The inner distribution of the offices should be in a way that management office can be isolated on case of emergency

ACCESS CONTROL

Area Access Control: An effective control system should be in effect for offices and factory facilities to identify visitors and allow them to be escorted to the required offices. In high threat periods, there should be periodical inspections of vehicles and personnel in the areas.

A physical barrier should be built through the entry track to prevent the access before being properly checked by the guards. If the office or factory is part of a more complex facility, in which access responsibility is shared, procedures must be reviewed and formalized among other area occupants or buildings.

Executive Office Access Control: The executive offices must be placed in a way that it is impossible for the visitor to gain entry without passing through the secretary's office.

Auxiliary Security Systems: Depending on the offices distribution, the possibilities to install access restriction and assault-intruder-office-protection auxiliary security systems should be consider, those measures may include the use of cable TV (CCTV), intercom system, electronics locks, etc.; these must be placed on the entry area perimeter as well as the executive offices' entries.

VIGILANT PERSONNEL

If vigilant personnel are hired, its abilities should be proportional to payment and environmental conditions. Two competent and well-trained guards might be more valued than six incompetent guards. Their abilities must include:

- Access control

- Perimeter patrol (including perimeter gate-damage searching)

- All area locking procedure

- Staff and vehicle inspections

- Building check in case of bomb threat

- Emergency reactions

The security instructions regarding working times, responsibilities and accident report procedures must be delivered to each security staff.

EMERGENCIES

All personnel must have established procedures on how to act in emergencies, for example: fire, bomb threat, armed assault, etc. The procedures must cover all types of emergency communications.

SECURITY INSTRUCTIONS

All personnel must be instructed on the following:

- Actions on fire or intruder alarms

- Evacuation procedures

- Access control

- Telephone procedures

- Confidential information protection

These instructions must be hard-copied as an office security manual.

SECURITY WITH GROUND TRANSPORTATION (kidnaps)

INTRODUCTION

Experience shows that the most vulnerable time for any potential kidnapping action is when moving from home to work. Thus, transportation security has become the most demanding of all personal security aspects, and requires constant surveillance of all basic rules.

A great many murders and kidnappings have taken place when the potential victim is walking or when he is getting in or out of his vehicle. The majority have taken place when the victim was inside the vehicle.

TRIPLE CARE WITH TRANSPORT SECURITY

Dissuasion: Most kidnappers have changed their intention of any planned victim solely because of that person's travel precautions when in an automobile, making him a "difficult" target. Therefore, dissuasion is a most valuable security procedure when dealing with transportation.

Case: A good example happened on Guatemala in 1980. A woman knew that her captors had planned originally to kidnap her brother. However, through surveillance, they knew that he travelled at irregular times and was well guarded, making him an unacceptable and difficult target, so they decided to leave him.   Regrettably, the kidnappers looked upon his sister. She admitted that she always travelled on regular schedules, and that she didn't take any precautions. It was really an error that cost 4 million dollars. However, it must be stated that no protection gives 100% protection, especially of it is a military kind assault.

Acknowledge the danger: If kidnappers plan on hitting a road victim, they will need certain amount of surveillance on it, generally for a long time. If they do not have special internal information, this will give an opportunity to the victim to be alert and to detect that he is under surveillance and to take precautions.

Carlos Marighella, the late Brazilian guerrilla leader, wrote on his "Mini Manual de Guerrilla Urbana" (Urban Guerilla Mini Manual): "Do a recognisance on the field, the study and opportunity of the routes is that important that omitting it would be like stabbing on the dark".

Case: Sir Geoffrey Jackson, the British ambassador in Uruguay on 1971, observed that he was being watched and notified to the Foreign Britain Office in London about it. However, for unknown reasons, he didn't take any safety measures and was kidnapped and held hostage.

Evasion: An alert chauffeur can detect and avoid possible ambush areas, so if an attack is to occur, he must know how to best react to avoid the kidnappers.

Case: In Cerdeña, in February of 1981, Luigi Colm was driving along the road, when a tree on the road hid several armed men who confronted him. A quick and steady reaction allowed him to withdraw from the ambush, and although being fired upon, he could escape.

VEHICLE SELECTION

The type of vehicle for regular use and the equipment it contains boosts security for the chauffeur and passengers. A vehicle is not only a means of transportation, fast and comfortable, but it can also mean, in case of an emergency, a protection from an ambush as well as a kidnapping.

Type of Vehicle: A regularly used vehicle should be of a common color and make and model. It must have ordinary license plates, and, most importantly, as it might be overlooked, it must be strong, safe, and fast, with good speed and providing a good driving view.

Basic Equipment for the Vehicle: All vehicles must have:

- At least three good rear-view mirrors

- Strong front and rear bumpers

- Solid locks, including window locks and a central lock system

- Locks on the hood, gas tank, and trunk

- Safety belts on all seats, the insert bobbin easy-to-use type

- A good spare tire, a spare gas container, a first aid kit, and a towing cable.

Vehicle modifications: All vehicles must be unnoticeably modified to have:

- A two-wave antenna radio

- Siren, with an inner foot-switch for use in an ambush

- Front reinforced bumpers

- An additional rear-view mirror for the front passenger

- Bullet proof windows and windshields

- Special, flat-rolling tires, to roll when deflated (or cube-security-bands)

- An anti-fire gas tank

- Shaded windows to prevent the passenger from being sighted

- Armored chassis and gas injectors or fume pots, placed as an anti-ambush precaution.

- An small pocket gun, sawed inside the front seat

- An alarm against tampering with an interior indicator

CHAUFFEURS

Chauffeurs must be trusted persons; therefore, they must be carefully examined before being hired. It is not enough that he knows how to drive, they must also be competent on: inspection and car check, motor maintenance, electric circuits, and tires, and he must know evasive and fast driving techniques.

Case: The kidnap of Miss Rehén Al Hasithi, of 12 years old, a former Saudi Arabia General's daughter, occurred in London. Scotland Yard arrested two men when the picked up the 150000 pounds ransom. One of them was the chauffeur. However, this is a "sub-fudged" case yet, that is why no further comments can be made on the chauffeur's role.

Case: April 1980, Naples, Francisco Coppela was kidnapped after being road-ambushed, where his car was forced to stop by two other vehicles. His chauffeur, who apparently failed to detect the danger and to take evasive maneuvers, allowing the car to be pushed off the road, was driving Coppela. A more alert chauffeur could have prevented this to happen.

Chauffeurs must be well trained and must practice routine and emergency procedures when:

- Garage parking.

- Routine procedures, for example, parking, dropping and picking up passengers.

- Emergency procedures, for example, car failures, aggressive and non-aggressive pursuit responses, and kidnap attempts.

- Pre-established urgency signaling implementations, among chauffeurs and passengers.

ROUTE SELECTION

The most frequent routes are between the house and office, between the house and store and school routes.
Despite the difficulties present in determining new routes, the routes must be selected based on the following criteria:

- Do not always use direct routes. For regular routes, there must be at least three to pick from.

- When possible, avoid vulnerable spots on the contrary keep extreme vigilance. Such vulnerable spots include: traffic lights, road workers, and shopping malls, with a lot of people, principal avenue yields and railroad crossings.

- Try to use double vehicle ways, free ways, and main roads when the traffic is fast.

- Avoid driving during peak hours; avoid obscure areas and dimmed spots, and danger areas.

- Familiarize yourself, with police stations, security forces and hospitals among the routes, for example, potential "safe refuges".

ROUTE PREPARATIONS AND PROCEDURES

- Always instruct the chauffeur with the route to follow, do not let him make the choice.

- Avoid the routine on route selection, as well as on the time. Being unpredictable is your best defense.

- Call before hand to your private secretary, using a coded signal to tell the route to be taken. Do the same when returning.

- Check the gas level to make sure you have at least half a tank.

- Do not overweight the car; an overweighed car cannot be driven in an evasive or defensive way.

- Before starting, readjust al mirrors carefully, fasten your seat belts, lock all doors and shut all windows (especially on crowded areas), if necessary for ventilation, the windows can be open 5 cm at tops.

- Heat the motor before leaving the garage and check car communication.

- Check brakes and guidance system before going on a public road.

- Make sure the road is cleared.

ROUTE PROCEDURES

- Keep the distance between your vehicle and the vehicle in front, especially when stopping, this allows you to have a maneuvering space if anything happens or if the front vehicle stops for repairs. As a general rule, when stopping you must always be able to see the front car's rear bumper.

- Stay on the furthest or middle tracks, especially when there is heavy traffic, this way it is harder to be pulled over.

- Travel in convoy with friends if possible.

- Stay focused at all time and check your rear view mirror constantly.

- Be alert watching for other vehicle surveillance

- Do not pick up anybody nor open windows or doors to strangers.

ACTIONS TO TAKE FOR DEPARTURES AND ARRIVALS

Departures:

- When leaving some place, survey the surroundings carefully before leaving the nearby establishment areas and approach your parked vehicle with caution.

- When departing from a garage where your car has spent the night, be more careful and watchful. It is better to inspect all streets before getting on the car.

- Check the car and the area around it for forceful attempts of entry signs, if anything catches your attention have your car checked out by a qualified person and make a competent explosives search.

- When starting the motor, continue to survey, especially when backing out the vehicle.

Arrivals:

- As you approach the parking area, slow down and carefully search in every direction.

- Park the car, keep the motor on and search again. Be prepared to accelerate and leave.

- If everything is fine, lock the car and check all doors (there might be a child's lock that could confuse you)

PARKING/GARAGE

- Any unwatched car must be locked all the time

- Do not park at sight, for your movements can to be seen easily. Park facing out for a quick departure

- Do not ever park on the same spot outside your office, club, favorite store, restaurant, etc. avoid a personal parking lot for it is an invitation for kidnapping

- Put your car on a garage that can be locked, at all time if possible.

- The garage must have a covered exit to the house

- Do not delay on entry; the garage must open as soon as possible.

VEHICLE MAINTENANCE

Good vehicle maintenance is essential to ensure a safe functional vehicle. However, due to occupants' vulnerability during travel, a car can be wrongly manipulated in a way to help a criminal.

- If possible, the chauffeur should do the all of the vehicle's servicing.

- A special maintenance must be coordinated by the chauffeur with the proper mechanic workshop and register the vehicle under the chauffeur's name.

- The vehicle must be delivered and picked up by a third party, preferably by the chauffeur.

- The owner must check the vehicle when returned, especially the inside of it, to check for tracking, guidance, or listening devices.

- The owner must carefully examine the workshops and decide which one will the chauffeur use.
- The radio should be taken out before delivering the vehicle to the service workshop.

EMERGENCY ENROUTE PROCEDURES

Vehicle Trouble:

- Move the vehicle from the road immediately, this will avoid a traffic jam and therefore won't call any attention

- Establish communication as soon as possible, informing about:
    Your exact location and possible means of contact (for example, cellular phone or a fixed one).
    Cause of aviary and if you'll need help.
    If you do not need help, how much time will you take to fix the aviary?.
    Steps to follow after repairs (for example, communicate again and/or continue with the planned route, check the time taken).

- If you are not able to do the vehicle repair, if there isn't a safe nearby place, well constructed, where to stay and wait, stay in the vehicle with all the doors locked and wait for help.

Non-aggressive Pursuit:

By definition, a non-aggressive pursuit can be a car followed up by another vehicle at a distance and with one or two occupants. It is objective can be to check your routine, discover your destination, your residence, or garage location. Your actions must be directed to:

- Verify that you are being followed by leaving the route and returning again,   following the same route.

- Drive normally to avoid any offensive action against you.

- Inform someone, giving a description as detailed as possible.

- Continue to your destination, and go to the safest near refuge (police station, or military outpost, a great hotel, hospital or government institution).

- Once inside your safe refuge, communicate again; give any other details, including location.

- Watch carefully before continuing your travel.

Aggressive Pursuit:

By definition one or two cars with two or more men in each one, that have approached, close and fast. Their intention is to force an ambush.

- Inform someone immediately.

- Proceed at top speed (with horn blowing) to the nearest safe refuge.

- Upon arrival, inform to the police, the family, and business associates and be prepared for a press reaction. A false kidnap statement may cause a real attempt to occur.

Kidnap attempt (ambush)

- It is vital to keep the car in movement

- To evade a blocked road:

- Drive through the middle of the road or near the sidewalk

- Hit the blocking car off the road, if it just requires an easy push and if it is improbable that your car stops because of the impact

- Retreat and runaway from the scene (if available drop a smoke cloud).

- Use a siren or horn (and smoke if possible).

- Avoid the use of fire guns, unless it is absolutely necessary. Be aware of the reprisal of gunfire.

Priority Principles:

As road traveling is the most dangerous movement for any potential victim, it requires constant preparation and surveillance to detect kidnappers, but to also detect and avoid the danger when close.

AUTOMOVILE INSPECTION - EXPLOSIVES

DETONATION OF EXPLOSIVES:

Explosive devices can be detonated inside or on a car in a variety of ways, these include:

a. **From the battery**
On lights (especially directional lights)
Horn

b. **From the ignition system**
Connected to: the ignition
The radio
The intermittent lights (indicators)

c. **Through the vehicle's own generated heat**
Radiator
Tail pipe
Moto

d. **Pressure activated interrupters**
Under the seats
Under the carpet
Under the car tires, especially when the car is about to move

e. **Triggering interrupters**
Under books, magazines
Under heavy objects

f. **Inclination activated interrupters:** A car on a slope (fixed to the chassis, etc.)

g. **Delayed mechanisms:** Placed anywhere inside or outside of the car.

PRECAUTIONS - SECURITY

Ignition key: Make sure the ignition key is on your possession and that the vehicle is not started before the inspection is over

PRELIMINARY VEHICLE CHECK-EXTERNAL ANDINTERNAL (VIEWING THROUGH THE WINDOWS)

Make a quick visual exam of the car, external and internal through the windows, do not touch anything

Walk around the car looking for anything abnormal, especially near the tires on the road

- Search for hit signals on the doors

- Look over the chassis, searching for any strange material (cables, etc.), especially around the motor cover.

- Look through the car windows, the windshield and the back windows for any strange object or familiar object that may be found on a different position from the one before leaving the vehicle or from those normally placed like

- Again, looking through the window, pay attention to the directional lights

- Look under the vehicle, looking for any strange material fixed on the chassis, on the tail pipe, etc., or placed under the tire fram

NOTE: All the inspections above need to be made safely but as quickly as possible.

PRELIMINARY VEHICLE CHECK-MOTOR AND TRUNK

- Open the passenger's door softly until you feel the first latch. If there are no signs of strange wires or other suspicious materials, open the door widely and leave it open. DO NOT ENTER THE CAR.

- From the front passenger's seat, check to see if there is anything abnormal on the driver's door, pay special attention to door handles.

- Open the driver's door softly until you feel the first latch. Check for any strange wires, open the door widely and leave it open.

- Without putting any pressure on the seats or carpets, release the hood lock.

- Approach the hood of the vehicle and search under the hood lifting. Check again for wires, etc., open it until you feel the first latch. Check again for wires or strange materials and the open the hood completely.

- Rapidly survey for any strange objects.

- Disconnect the battery

- Open the trunk carefully, keeping weight over the cover and searching for wires or any other strange materials. Open the trunk completely.

- Examine the interior of the trunk searching for strange objects.

NOTE: All inspections mentioned above must be done in a safe way but as quickly as possible. If there is any suspicious object during any of the steps above, DO NOT continue the inspection. Call the experts.

DETAILED VEHICLE CHECK

When doing this detailed exam, do not press on any seat or stand in any way until safety is assured.

Flashlights and mirrors can be used to check on dark areas or inaccessible areas.

This detailed check must include:
- The motor area
- The inside of the car
  Under the seats
  Under the carpets
  On the shelves
  On the ashtrays
  On the glove compartment
- Trunk
  Spare tire
  Tool box
  Any box
- Under the car:
  Add, especially to the chassis and the tail pipe, and the wheel rings.

ACTIONS TO TAKE IN CASE OF FINDING AN OBJECT

YOU MUST NOT
- Touch it
- Try to move it

YOU MUST
- Call the proper authorities

TELEPHONE PROTECTION

A considerable amount of confidential information can be unintentionally told through the phone to a person with extortion or kidnap intentions. As they do not intend to reveal their identity, it is nearly impossible to detect the calls efficiently.

USEFUL INFORMATION FOR TERRORISTS AND CRIMINALS

The kind of information concerning a potential victim that is useful for a terrorist or criminal includes:
- Location: If the target is at a specific place

- Time: Time expected for the target to leave or arrive

- Future plans

DATA EXTRACTION

All office personnel, particularly management secretaries and phone operators, must be aware of the ways data can be extracted from them when talking on the phone.
Family members also must be aware of this. Everybody must be constantly on guard.

- **Location:** A direct question to determine the location of the target or where he could be found.

- **Appointment:** A false appointment is concerted at a time and specific place.

- **Wrong number:** The terrorist or criminal gives as an excuse he had dialed the wrong number when the target responds.

- **Help call:** The person calling wishes to contact the target urgently for very familiar or sympathetic reasons.

- **Partial knowledge:** The person calling gives false information expecting to be corrected by the target.

- **Incorrect information:** Information about the management obtained from the personnel who are not directly involved.

- **Adulation:** Information obtained via the secretary or operator through flattery.

ANSWERING PROCEDURES

Whenever it is possible, an intermediary must be used. In an office, it could be a receptionist, telephone operator, or secretary. At home, it could be a trusted personnel member. The duty of the intermediary is to act as a filter for all incoming calls and insuring that the target's voice is not recognized. When answering the phone, the intermediary must be reserved:

- Allow the person calling to initiate the conversation.

- Do not offer any information.

- Be kind but firm.

- Identify the person calling.

- If the identification is not ratified immediately, ask for the telephone number of the person calling.

- Nicely ask the person calling to hold on while the employer checks the identification.

- If the identification is not ratified and there is a motive to suspect, ask for the reason of the call.

- Explain to the person calling that his/her message will reach the person in charge or the intermediary.

AUXILIARY TELEPHONE SYSTEMS

Many systems and procedures can be used so as to increase phone security, these include:

Confidential telephone number

- A confidential telephone number that is not listed in the phone book. If possible keep a record of the people who know this number.

- Make sure that the phone number is not placed on the front part of the telephone.

- According to circumstances, register your home phone numbers as those of an enterprise.

Answering machine

The answering machine was especially designed to record those phone messages when there is nobody home. Alternatively, this device can be used as any normal recorder so the user can comfortably listen to the message.

Recording

A simple recording of all conversations is possible.

What to and not to do
What to do:

Have a prepared procedure in order to respond.
Be firm but kind
Identify
Ask for the name and phone number if unknown.

What not to do:

Inform the caller of the location of the employer.

PHONE THREATS

RECEPTION AND REACTION

All industrial and commercial organizations need to be prepared to receive threatening calls. These calls can be related to extortion, kidnapping, or bombing and, at least at the beginning, they should be considered genuine.
A well-defined preparation is required to ensure the most information from the caller and to

assure the procedures to be implemented because of personnel and property security. Certain people must be assigned to act as required and accordingly to the specific instructions on receiving such calls.

The following sequence of actions must be applied to have effect on the phone threats.

Preparation:

- Education and personnel drills.

- Co-ordination with authorities

- Establish a written emergency procedure

Reception:

- Reception of the call and information obtaining

- Registry of the information

- Report immediately and safely the information to the people named to act.

Reaction:

- Threat evaluation

- Implementation of an emergency plan

TYPES OF CALLS

Threatening calls received through the phone line, can be of three types:

- Mockery - made by a mischief

- Fake - deliberate attempts to cause disorganization or to observe the company's reactions.

- Genuine

CALLS SHOULD NEVER BE IGNORED BUT ALWAYS ACT AS EXPECTED

Surely the threat itself will be as a bomb threat, but the assigned personnel who receive those calls must be aware of the possibilities of an extortionist or kidnappers' demands.

Education and Personal Practice

It must be a generally known task to identify which phones will be used mostly for phone threats. Most often, these extensions will be registered at the central office.

People who call certainly do not want to spend any second waiting to be transferred to an extension. That is why any person answering must be familiarized with the accorded procedures.

It is recommended that the personnel train for receiving such calls.

There is a verification list to cover the reception of a threatening call. It has been made adequately to deal with any kind of threat. This verification list must be made in the native tongue of two phone users and must be kept at hand near the phones. The users must practice until it is a natural reaction to utilize the verification list when receiving a threat call. In high-risk areas, the importance of installing a recording machine on the telephone lines should be considered.

All personnel must be taught to keep their offices as clean and orderly as possible. There must be a minimum of books and papers, the drawers must be locked, and the trashcans must be emptied regularly.

Coordination with the authorities

The security chief or the person named for those obligations must coordinate with the corresponding authorities. The next aspects should be considered:

- Location and details for contacting with the local emergency services, especially the nearest bomb squad.

- A trained squad assistance and availability for identification and reaction towards explosive devices.

- Reconnaissance made by the bomb-evacuation squad to familiarize them with the company's facilities.

EMERGENCY PROCEDURES

Simple written instructions are required to ensure an immediate and effective response after the reception of a phone threat. These must include:

- **Plant safety measures:**
  Who will order to secure the plant?
  Where will be located the control zone?
  Where will communication with the control zone be established?
  Who will direct access points?
  Who will be allowed to the exit areas?

- **Measure to inspect the plant:**
  Who will order and direct the search?
  From where it'll be controlled?
  Who will make the inspection? (If at all possible, all area personnel must be used)
  How will the inspection teams inform that an area is cleared?
  NOTE: Plant inspection can be made, on certain circumstances, without evacuation.

- **Measures to evacuate the plant:**
  Who will order and direct the evacuation?
  From where will it be controlled?
  How will it be organized?
  Which routes will be used?

Where will be the gathering points?
Who will check and declare a clear area?
Who will control people's entry to the gathering areas?
What measures should be taken for essential/dangerous machinery?
Who will in charge to provide a nominal updated list of main workers and their work places?
How will be the return to their workstations?

- **Measures to face in case of a fire:**
  Which one is the alarm and how's it set on?
  Who will take control?
  Who will call the firemen, to which number and how?
  Who will receive and guide the firemen, to where?
  Who will be on the fire squad for the plant?
  What is the location of the fire equipment for the plant?
  Where are the main and alternative water faucets?
  Are there any toxic/dangerous substances and how to face the problem?
  Are evacuation plans needed?

- **Accident measures:**
  Who will notify about accidents?
  Who will call the Hospital/Ambulance?
  Who will receive the Ambulance and where?
  Are there First Aid personnel on the plant?
  Is there any medical equipment, if so, where is it?

RECEPTION OF A PHONE THREAT

If the preparation, indicated on previous paragraphs was made, then the persons receiving the threatening call may be able not to avoid having that first normal panic reaction and try to extract from the calling person all possible information. There are two types of information.

- **Peripheral**
  Date and time of call
  Call time
  Phone used
  Details on the calling person (male, female, old, young, accent, tone of voice, state of mind, impression)
  Background sounds

- **Text:** The calling person might have in mind (possibly as a textbook), the threat to be made. The task of the receiving person will not be only to retrieve the message but also to extract the most possible additional information. It is recommended focusing on the following:

- **Priority**
  WHEN will the bomb explode and will the extortion threat will be followed through with?
  WHERE is the bomb located/? To whom is the extortion threat directed?
  HOW is the bomb? (Size)

- **Attitude:**
  Important information can be acquired if the call is correctly received. The calling person might be waiting to cause panic with his call, and he is not psychologically prepared to be answered upon bay a calm, positive person.

PROCEDURES AFTER THE CALL

Once the call has been made, the first thing to be done is to register all the information on the verification list. Once this has been done, the receiving person must have an immediate meeting, face to face, with the security chief or his named assistant, to ensure that they are aware of the call and that they are informed about the details of it.
It is important that this is kept confidential and that no one knows about the call until the boss has decided the course of actions.

Evaluation of the Threat: The first task of the security chief or named person is to evaluate the phone-made threat and to decide the course of actions to take. The following must be considered:

- Degree of the normal threat

- Previously similar incidents

- Analysis of the call made:
  Content and threat
  Questions to the phone operator

Emergency Bomb Threat Plan Implementation

- **If the threat neither is nor considered too serious, the following must be done:**
  - Make an inspection, using the specially "named" people.
  - The company personnel can or cannot be informed (this lays on the discretion of the security chief)

- **If the threat is considered genuine, the next should be done:**
  - Inform the bomb evacuation unit (to the correct number)
  - Establish a control zone
  - If time allows it, do a search, using trained people
  - Evacuate the local (the assigned personnel to check that the areas are cleared must inform to the control zone)
  - Move all the personnel to a safe distance (at least 100 meters). However, remember that your secure area's location might be known by the aggressor, who may have placed a second device in that area; therefore, you must be sure that the area is cleared of items such as trashcans, pots, or any such thing to place a bomb.
  - Secure the perimeter
  - Confirm that al personnel is present
  - Brief shortly to the authorities when arrived, and have the inspectors are hand for questions, is there is any.

Extortion

Extortion can be combined with fire threats, premeditated gunshots, kidnappings, or other acts. Once identified the type of threat, all security precautions must be intensified. If police investigation does not find anything, the security precautions must be on alert until a management decision is consciously made to reduce such measures by recommendation and accordingly to specific situation circumstances. However, if there is still doubt, it is recommended taking the most secure measure even if it brings inconvenient.

REPORTING A THREATENING PHONE CALL

Date and Time: Your name
Ask the following:

1. When will the bomb explode? / Was that threat made?
2. Where is the bomb? / To whom is the threat?
3. Describe the bomb (size).
4. Keep the person calling talking and ask: Who is he? Whom does he represent?
5. Why is he making this threat?
6. What are the exact words the calling person has made?
   a. How did he sound?
   b. Male/female, young/old, calm/frightened. Educated/hostile, accent
   c. Tone of voice
   d. Phone noise/impediments
   e. Did he sound familiar?
   f. Other impressions

NOTE: As soon as the call ends, and once this form is completed, call the next people on the list:
   a. Telephone Mr. ……………………..
   b. Telephone Mr. ……………………..
   c. Telephone Mr. ……………………..

IDENTIFICATION AND HANDLING OF MAIL AND PACKAGES THAT MAY HAVE BOMBS

People who handle the mail must be familiarized with the bomb-mail features. The use of x-rays or metal detectors is an invaluable aid in this field

EXPLOSIVE LETTERS

In practice, any letter less than 8 mm wide cannot have a Highly Explosive (HE) bomb. However, it may have an arson or acid device. Any letter more than 8 mm wide may have a HE bomb.
Such mail, received through the mail, should function like one of the following:
- Opening the package

- Removing a thread or scotch (at any time)
- Removing its content

Plus, the letter, especially those delivered by other medium (for example, by hand), may function with delayed mechanisms (for example, without being opened or moved).

Explosive letters are generally stiff and difficult to bend.

DO NOT TRY TO BEND IT

Following we list some features that an explosive device can have:
- Smell like almond
- Any powder-color spots
- Oil spots or leaks
- A small hole on the exterior of the letter

The alternatively delivered mail that is not delivered by the post office must be treated with extreme suspicion.
- The stamps may indicate known terrorist-like places.
- The mail must be open away from the face or eyes

ACTIONS TO TAKE WITH SUSPICIOUS MAIL

YOU MUST NOT: Crush it or intervene in any way
YOU MUST NOT: Place it on water or any other liquid
YOU MUST: Examine it at possible, with x-rays or a metal detector
YOU MUST: Place it on a DRY spot and away from glasses or metal, the place must be chosen accordingly to the following:
- On the yard or a reserve area:
- Inside a box with cover made preferably of wood or plastic and placed as far as possible from the personnel.
- On an inhabited basement
- On an isolated room: Preferably without windows, and if there is any, they must be opened. Personnel must not work or be on a 25-meter area
YOU MUST: Call the pertinent authorities

EXPLOSIVE PACKAGES
All packages can have a HE bomb.
All post office delivered packages may work as previously stated for letters
Other medium delivered packages (for example, by hand), may work as HE letters
Packages received from unknown sources or unspecified, must be treated as suspicious

MARK THE MAIL THAT IS BEEN EXAMINED BY X-RAYS/METAL DETECTOR
The words:
"Passed x-ray exam the day .... (date)"
Metal Detector

It must be sealed of passed the exams successfully (The words "X-rays" or "Metal Detector" can be suppressed of more appropriate)

HOSTAGE SURVIVAL

HOSTAGE PREPARATION

The wish is to prepare the potential victims for the kind of troubles and conditions they will face in case of being kidnapped. Hostages have been held many months at thought conditions. The shock that a middle-aged business executive suffers, can be hard, particularly if he is not prepared

The most difficult problem the victim faces is the fear to the unknown. A basic education program can lessen this apprehension and certainly is a standard practice for military units who are "more likely to be captured".

THE KIDNAP

As a general rule in all kidnap attempts, it is not recommended to escape, at least if there is a clear chance of success. On any other cases, heroism can lead to dead by a terrorist and/or nervous or poorly trained criminal.

Case: Mr. Curtis Cutter, General Consul of the USA in Porto Alegre, Brazil, was driving his way home with his wife. After finishing a meal, on April 1970, when they suffered a kidnap attempt. He accelerated toward the group that was trying to block the road an escaped with minor injuries.

After the capture and especially when on the initial route toward the kidnapper's hideout, the victim must be alert and as calm and aware as possible. He must take mental notes of anything that could help the police in their efforts to capture the kidnappers after being set free, for example:
- All movement details, including hours, distances, directions, sounds and signs (this would be difficult because the victim would probably be blindfolded or drugged)
- Description and features of his captors
- The surrounding's description, including any other place he could be taken to.

PRISON

The "people's prison" or hideouts, vary enormously. The common factor is that the hostage will be totally isolated and it is probable that he will not know any other person, if they are well masked.

Terrorist and/or criminals generally prefer houses in quiet places, sometimes little workshop factories, or far off-the-beaten track cottages or abandoned buildings. If they are professionals, they will chose a place with covered access from the garage leading to the main building and with a good escape route. The victim can be held in a basement or in a dugout cell under the building from where the access is through a camouflaged trap (sometimes it is a booby trap). The prison will be probably dark, moist and dirty. The sleeping, washing and toilet features may be very primitive.

TREATMENT AFTER THE CAPTURE

Life after the capture may be difficult and unpleasant, particularly on contrast with the comfy way of living of the hostage. This may lead to severe moral troubles that can overcome to mental and physical illness. Other additional problems can be set intentionally:

- The capture made by a criminal gang can be followed by brutality or abandonment, but may not include the related political issues with the kidnaps made by terrorists. However, it is essential for the victim to keep his dignity and self-respect to avoid impairment during captivity.

- The terrorist kidnap surely will be followed by interrogation and indoctrination. Generally, the traditional physical torture is not used, though there are ways of equal effectiveness and as subtle: the physical torture adds a motive for hatred towards the captors and therefore more resistance. However, when the victim reaches his limits, it is probably he will tell his captors what they want to hear and not necessarily the truth. "Truth drugs" will reduce resistance and void inhibitions, bet they are in no way a relief for the interrogator. An overdose may cause the victim to reveal a lot of nonsense, and if the victim's strong, he can resist a minor dose.

The actual interrogation methods have mental disorientation, mainly induced by sleep deprivation, humiliation, degradation, noises and light periods alternated with total silence and darkness. Pavlovian techniques are also used to reinforce the dependency of a prisoner and his captor. The first gets to depend upon his captor, as a child depends on his mother to any kind of help, food or comfort. Hostage situations, in which the victim and captors have the same problems and are threaten by a common "enemy", have ended with a common sympathy and opinion likeness.

In Stockholm where the police in a bank vault cornered the criminals along with their hostages, a strong bond among captors and hostages held for a long time after the incident ended. The hostages where found in a situation in which the police were considered the enemy and the captors were the protectors. The development of such situation depends on the communication between the parts, and the share of fear and privation. It is probably that this will happen in a kidnapping.

BEHAVIOR AFTER THE KIDNAP

Nervous prostration after the capture is a very grave psychological problem. It is probable that is worst for an executive or even for a plane pilot when the capture is completely unexpected. This carries a serious trauma caused by a total change of situation.

All in which the victim had faith has become chaos and confusion. The captors will have a superior position and domination and the victim will experience a profound depression.

It is important that the victim recognizes this situation and that he takes the necessary measures to reaffirm his self esteem at first chance. The hostage must do conscious efforts to keep his physical and mental health during captivity. It is useful a self-discipline despite (and because of) the environment or an inactive life. A strict schedule must be help as well as order and cleanliness.

The relation with the captors on this situation must be taken with humor or with a boring and tedious cooperation. It is not advisable to have a strong resistance or to abuse them. Most prisoners have found useful to identify priorities during captivity:

- The principles by which they are prepared to die: They are certain actions that are completely unacceptable, and the captive must mentally prepare to refuse any of those demands (for example, to betray a family member would be on this category)

- Situations to which he must resist to for they are so degrading as unpleasant.

- Situations, on which, despite being unpleasant or unusual, however, they do not break the hostages well being, must be accepted.

These categories can include doing the biological functions on a small corner and within the kidnappers' sight. Physical health will be maintained by eating all the presented food, even if it is repulsive and poorly attractive, doing a regular series of exercises although confined to a small cell.

Identifying and attaching to a valor system and establishing priorities to cooperation and resistance will keep the mental health. The mind must be kept active in the most convenient way for the individual but a conscious effort must be needed to achieve it. Not all advantages are for the captors. It is important for the captors to remember that the hostage is to be advertised, and it is possible that he will assure them against the police attack, and that the hostage is the reason that will bring them a great ransom. A dead victim will increase their guilt and, of course, the ransom will not be awarded to them.

Some prisoners have passed long periods composing mental music, planning escapes, writing poetry, or designing the ideal house on which they will live when set free. It is healthy to prepare a mental activity toward a future situation when the victim is freed. If there're writing materials, it can be of great help, but a lot can be achieved using just the mental activity.

It is important that the hostage does not argue about the actions that his family would do his work, or his friends on the company. Such arguments can only jeopardize negotiations for if he were to be set free. Also, it is necessary to caution to not identify any family member or friend. As mentioned previously, when held after the kidnapping, there must not be an escape attempt if it is not probably to succeed

AGAINST THE KIDNAPPERS

To be kidnapped is one of the most impressionable and risky experiences a person can suffer; to not know if you will be killed, tortured or how long your captivity will be. This risk is the most fearful, even more so than an assassination or another violation.

We do admit that there is little a person can really do if they are confronted with a situation such as this; it will not be easy to prepare before a violent event like a kidnapping.

If you or someone you are familiar with would have the unfortunate situation of becoming a kidnapping victim, it is important to remember that it is the attitude that you assume that may determine the difference if you live or how you are treated during the kidnapping.

In the initial phases of the kidnapping the captors may demonstrate a little nervousness and excitedness. If this be the case, the kidnappers may be capable of killing the victim because they were not able to remain calm and believed they did not control the situation.

The kidnappers and/or terrorists with the purpose of gaining a ransom from the kidnapping, will immediately abuse the victim with verbal assaults, threatening death, showing their power over the victim, and issuing religious insults, all with the purpose of destroying the moral of the victim.

It is important to preserve the calmness and do not resist the captors so you may increase the possibility of appearing weaker physically than them.

CHAPTER III

PERSONAL SECURITY PROCEDURES

PROCEDURES TO ADOPT IN CASE OF RECEIVING CORRESPONDENCE

The following are general guidelines of the procedures to be adopted in case of receiving any correspondence that may contain explosive devices.

Generally, the common type of bomb-letter uses a plastic-moldable explosive, which is placed in flat giving the look of a piece of cardboard paper.

When the envelope is torn apart, a small spring is freed and hits the trigger, which is a little bigger than an aspirin tablet, which detonates.

The entire device can weigh less than an ounce (28 grams) and be approximately 3 mm. wide, but can kill or wound a person within 6.5 ft (2 m). Similar devices can be placed in books, packs of cigarettes, boxes, parcels, etc., so all of the mail must be carefully examined.

To detect a bomb-letter or parcel, it is enough to act with common sense, along with these precautions that will help safe your life.

VERIFICATION LIST

External look

- Oil or grease spots on the envelope (exudation of the plastic explosive)

- Inks, particularly red and blue may ooze staining the envelope.

- The use of tapes or extra seals or other elements such as strings or cords.

- A peculiar smell, particularly if it smells like almond.

- Wires, stripes of metal that come out of the envelope or are glued.

- You can sense springs to the upper and lower sides. When turning the envelope slightly, you can notice loose pieces of metal.

Weight

- Heavier than usual to its size

- Uneven distribution of weight.

Stiffness

- Bigger than normal

- Notice its flexibility on the top, bottom and sides of the envelope (do not bend it too much)

Thickness

- Uneven and with lumps.

- For medium size envelopes, the thickness equivalent to a small book and slightly rigid.

- For large envelopes, an inch or more thick.

Address

- If the sender is unusual or unknown.

- If there is no sender's name or address.

- Incorrectly typed or handwritten

- Addressed to a personage, by name, degree, title or department inside the organization.

- The title or rank of the personage is incorrect

Handwriting

- Sealed with some of the usual seals: PERSONAL - CONFIDENTIAL - PRIVATE - URGENT

- Sealed with CERTIFIED - SPECIAL DELIVERY

- Misspelled words, particularly those of military use

- Strange handwriting style or different to the usual terminology

Stamps

- Use of more stamps than necessary

- Use of post seals from an unknown town, city or district (improbable)

EXPLOSIVE DEVICE PROCEDURES TO ADOPT IN CASE OF AN EXPLOSION OR FINDING OF AN

The following are general guidelines that should be adopted in case of an explosion or finding of an explosive device.

A terrorist bomb does not have a self-objective since it could be used to deviate security forces' attention to make them target of an ambush or other explosions of a bigger magnitude.

All actions to take should be cautious, considering at all times the possibility of other tricky actions, such as booby traps or ambushes.

Below there is a list of what personnel detecting an unexploded bomb MUST and MUST NOT do or when reaching the scene of an incident of an explosive device.

WHAT MUST BE DONE

- Establish a control headquarter, limiting a security area and coordinating with the authorities involved.

- Clear the area at least 500 ft (150 m) from the bomb. In the case of buildings, offices, dining rooms, and blocks, evacuate all personnel as quickly and orderly as possible beyond the security limits.

- Deviate all vehicle and people traffic in the zone.

- Gather credible eyewitnesses. Ones who saw the bomb, the make of vehicle, and the behavior and attitude at the control headquarter.

- In case of detention of any suspect individuals, proceed to interrogation.

- Call for the presence of the Special Operation Squad Personnel ready for deactivation.

- Clear the area, if possible of all flammable materials to avoid expansion of fire.

- Shut off the electricity in the area to avoid short circuits.

- Alert firemen and paramedics if necessary.

- Get as much information as possible about the incident.

- Secure the area in order to prevent any possible thieves, vandalism, or sabotage actions.

- Follow the Special Operation Squad chief's orders at his arrival.

- Treat people kindly. Do not give any type of information, and keep them away from the scene along the operation time.

WHAT MUST NOT BE DONE

- Do not touch or approach the bomb.

- Assume wrongly that an explosion means that the area is secure and that there will not be any more explosions.

- Allow any person to approach the bomb before the Special Operation Squad chief declares the area safe.

- Insist on "being taken along" with the deactivation squad to the operation.

- Allow the Special Operation Squad personnel to be photographed.

- Reveal:
  - The names of the Special Operation Squad personnel.
  - The nature of the bomb.
  - Any reason resulting in a malfunction of the bomb.
  - The techniques used to deactivate the bomb.

INFORMATION TO BE GIVEN TO THE CHIEF OF THE DEACTIVATION SQUAD AT HIS ARRIVAL

- Where the bomb is.

- What it looks like.

- When it was placed.

- What alert was given?

- Whether there are available eyewitnesses.

- Whether there are any suspects to interrogate.

- Who is securing the area?

- Whether there is any hostile or sabotage group in the area.

PROCEDURE IN CASE OF FINDING YOURSELF AS A HOSTAGE

Although there are no strict rules to apply to every hostage situation, the following are recommendations to be considered:

- Be optimistic. If the victim stays clam so will be the criminal. If you treat them with respect, then you could expect a similar attitude from the kidnappers.

- Follow their instructions; be cordial to the kidnappers.

- Do not anticipate your early freedom. Many kidnappings by terrorists last for months and sometimes years. Be self-protective for a long lasting abduction.
- A study of these rapture and kidnapping situations has demonstrated that if prolonged, the greatest probability is that the victim should be rescued or freed.

- Try to mentally focus on the place where you have been taken, if you have been blind fold, try to locate yourself, notice any special odors, sounds; many times this will give you hints of where you are, especially if your familiar to the area or city.

- Cultivate human relationships. Identify those kidnappers with whom you can communicate and try to establish a relationship with them. Do not allege nor argue, try to converse about neutral aspects.

- Talk normally. Avoid whispering when talking to other hostages.

- Avoid provoking your kidnappers, do not complain nor act deliberately or be uncooperative when dealing with a terrorist or others hostages.

- Do not deliberately turn your back on the terrorist, especially to the leader one.

- Do not reject any favor done by the terrorist (including foods, drinks, and tobacco.).

- Be yourself, no matter how long the hostage situation takes, keep up your personal hygiene, exercise regularly.

- Keep track of your time. Try to establish a daily routine, keep yourself and mind busy at all times.

- Set your place. Part of your daily routine would be to put in order the room; this will help you keep your time busy and self-respectful.

- Remember that all negotiations and plans are in progress, for your benefit.

- Calculate the possibilities of escape. If there is evidence that you will be killed at any time, it could be worth trying to escape.

- Be alert to all signs of the efforts of external rescue.

- Do not worry about your family, they have been informed, and are kept up to date about your situation and are being taken care of.

- Do not get desperate on answering questions about yourself, except if your position, charge or trip proposal results an additional threat to the terrorist.

- Lie on the floor or if possible stay down during a rescue operation.

- The hostages will not, under any circumstances, move towards the rescue squads, running or moving suddenly or unexpectedly. Rescue squads will not be able to note the hostages.

PROCEDURES TO FOLLOW WHEN RECEIVING BOMB THREATENING PHONE CALLS

Because of the nature of receiving a phone call threatening of a bomb, the position to adopt is to pay careful attention to the call, so as to obtain the most information from it in order to detect the device and have the signs that will allow identifying the persons involved.

To get such information, a format has been attached, and from its completion, it is possible to obtain de above-mentioned data.

PROCEDURES

- When receiving a "bomb threatening" phone call, the operator should remain calm, pay attention, listen to the information, not interrupt and write down the exact words of the person who called.

- It is advisable to wait until the person who is calling finishes giving the message. By the end of it, it is necessary to obtain information about the bomb and its location, asking the questions of the attached format.

- At the end of the communication, the sections of the format should be filled in according to the profile that the operator is capable of getting from the person who called, and proceed immediately to call security.

- It should be noted that if it were not really an attack, they would not have bothered calling, asking for information, and letting known their wish to save human lives.

FORMAT OF BOMB THREAT

QUESTIONS THAT MUST BE ASKED:

- When will the bomb go off?

- Where is the bomb located?

- What does it look like?

- What kind of explosive is it?

- Why was it set

MARK WHAT CORRESPONDS:

a) Source of the call
- ( ) Local
- ( ) Phone booth
- ( ) Long distance
- ( ) Undetermined

b) Voice
- ( ) Male
- ( ) Adult
- ( ) Strong
- ( ) Serious
- ( ) Hoarse
- ( ) High
- ( ) Female
- ( ) Juvenile
- ( ) Slow
- ( ) Joking
- ( ) Kind
- ( ) Intense

c) Words
- ( ) Quick
- ( ) Clear
- ( ) Stammering
- ( ) Unsure
- ( ) Slow
- ( ) Distortional
- ( ) Nasal
- ( ) Babbling

d) Accent
- ( ) Local
- ( ) Provincial
- ( ) Mountaineer
- ( ) Backwoods
- ( ) Foreign
- ( ) American

- ( ) European
- ( ) Static

e) Speech
- ( ) Good
- ( ) Poor
- ( ) Unpleasant

f) Background sound
- ( ) Music
- ( ) Festive
- ( ) Silence
- ( ) Voices
- ( ) Machinery
- ( ) Office equipment
- ( ) Street traffic
- ( ) Animals
- ( ) Trains
- ( ) Planes
- ( ) Other

g) Manners
- ( ) Calm
- ( ) Coherent
- ( ) Polite
- ( ) Rational
- ( ) Upset
- ( ) Incoherent
- ( ) Smiling
- ( ) Irrational
- ( ) Confident
- ( ) Premeditated
- ( ) Arrogant
- ( ) Nervous
- ( ) Emotional
- ( ) Drunk

ADDITIONAL INFORMATION

_____

DATE:_____ **TIME:**_____

RECEPTION PHONE NUMBER:_____

OPERATOR: _____

ACTIONS TO TAKE:

- Concluding the communication, fill in the above format and as soon as possible hand it in to the Security chief informing the news.

- Act calmly. Do not panic; remember that if it were not really an attack, they would not have bothered calling you.

PROCEDURES TO CONTROL OFFICE VISITORS

The following are procedures to adopt when having office visitors.

- A "Visitors Control Diary" is to be kept, signed by all visitors (which will be a proof of handwriting styles for graphology studies)

- Such Diary will be placed in a way that it will force visitors to bend over the security personnel, giving them the chance to a "visual check-up", in which they could observe any sharp belt folding or other projecting body, revealing the presence of hidden weapons.

- Briefcases should be checked since they could contain devices, visitors should open their briefcases on their laps. Opening them on the desk is not permitted.

- If the visitor is carrying packages, an area for placing such things is to be designated (security is demanded for it could explode.).

- It will not be allowed to drop any packaged before it is clear:
    - Where is it from?
    - Who sends it?
    - Is destination correct?

- You should be extremely cautious with the delivering person if they play a trick in order to leave the package, such as returning for something left in the vehicle or for confirming addresses.

- Do not attempt to examine a suspicious box or package, by-the-book procedures are to be followed.

- It should be remembered that terrorists commonly come in man-woman couples, so be careful if this happens to be the case.

- All visitors must show identification, including military or police dressed personnel.

PROCEDURES AND NORMS FOR MOBILIZATIONS SECURITY

The following are norms to orientate the adoption of precautions to be considered when moving or transiting.

Recent cases have demonstrated that most terrorist attacks, dealing with murders and kidnappings, have been carried out while the victim was moving or in transit.

VULNERABILITY ASPECTS

- The potential victim is at most danger when entering or going out from home or work.

- When the person is driving, he or she is generally concentrated on doing so, or talking with a companion or listening to the radio and is not at all alert to signs of an eventual attack.

- It is very important that the times and routes from home, business places, shopping or any other normally programmed trip, lack a defined pattern, becoming as unpredictable as possible.

CHOOSING THE VEHICLE

The models of the vehicles should be common (brand, model, color) to those in the market. If possible avoid using luxury cars since they are easily identifiable. They should not present stickers, signs, and plates that identify the owner.

MAINTENANCE AND CARE OF THE VEHICLE

If possible, vehicles should be appropriately maintained, especially security systems such as tires, brakes, etc. The gas tank always should be filled above halfway as it is not convenient to run out of gas during a terrorist attack. Install an additional side view mirror, fire extinguisher, alarm, emergency lights, first aid kit, and consider also polarizing the windows.

VEHICLE PARKING

A good practice is to lock all vehicle doors every time the vehicle is parked. By securing the vehicle at night, it should be kept in a garage with windows and doors closed. If you do not have a garage, leave the car parked near the front door, with the alarm system on and in a well-illuminated zone. This will help to watch out for any suspicious activity.

VEHICLE INSPECTION TECHNIQUES

Always inspect the vehicle before using it. Proceed as follows:

- Make sure the vehicle is closed and locked at all times (doors, hood, trunk, and gas tank)

    - Keep the inside ordered and clean so that unusual objects can be clear and easily seen.
    - Avoid leaving the car with no vigilance.
    - Stay alert in case of:
    - Unusual objects inside or around the vehicle.
    - Objects out of place.
    - External signs of lock or window breaking, etc.
    - Loose wires, electrical cords or electrical tapes.
    - Packages or bags left on top of the vehicle.
    - Removed dirt or ground around the car.

- Almond paste smell or other strong perfumes inside or around the car.

- If the vehicle has been left without vigilance, it should be inspected before using it, in the following sequence.

- Observe all the exterior parts of the vehicle.

- Watch through the windows

- Look around and under each tire and between the tire and the fender.

- Look under the vehicle (especially the gas tank, muffler and tail pipe.).

- Open the hood and watch the engine, check for the existence of cables, wires or rare packages.

- Open the trunk and watch for anything unusual.

DRIVERS (CHAUFFEURS)

If a driver is to be hired, get a young, healthy one. If possible, he must be trained in special security techniques. If a formal training is not available, train him yourself and make sure he keeps the standards.

The next are some of the rules if you have a driver:

- Establish a security signal with your driver, which will allow you to only take action if the signal is given.

- When getting in the car, make the driver keep your door open while you are at a certain distance of the car, this will let you see inside the vehicle to see there is no one hiding.

- If when leaving home, work or other places, you suspect anything wrong before getting in the car, use your shrewdness doing things such as looking at your watch, look for your keys in your pocket or anything similar but natural, and get back immediately to the building, lock the door and watch through a window to see what is going on and determine the danger.

- Be cautious enough if the driver is away unexpectedly.

- Let the driver know where you are heading to once the vehicle has started running. If it is extremely necessary to do it before running, just let him know the area. Take precautions with those programmed trips.

- Sit in the front seat, next to the driver. Remember that the right back seat is the VIP seat, and those using it are in someway important people.

DRIVING OR RIDING IN VEHICLES

These are some precautions to be considered when driving or riding in vehicles

- Dress civil clothes, in case you had to wear uniform (if military) wear an overcoat, do not wear hats or caps.

- If you have armed security personnel, they ought to be as discreet as possible, they will ride next to the driver and act like observers or vigilantes.

- When the car is in motion, seat belts are mandatory, doors and windows locked, windows can be open a maximum of two centimeters.

- All occupants must be alert to all movements around and along the way, including possible persecutions by other cars being these pickup trucks, vans, or motorcycles.

- Take precautions if you see cars or trucks by the sides of the road. If possible avoid passing by, especially if you observe people around such vehicles.

- When driving keep distant from the car in front and back in order to perform emergency maneuvers if necessary.

- Drivers must always avoid being deviated of the way by other cars, all the persons in the car should know the routes, and be alert to ambush situations.

- Use main streets and avenues, trips to distant places and especially in dark hours must be avoided. If it is entirely necessary, do it in a convoy.

- Keep track of police stations, hospitals, military headquarters and other security areas along the way, since these could be helpful if a problem shows up.

PURSUITS

Normally, pursuit does not mean an imminent attack, terrorists generally observe their victims for a while before they attack so they could establish their victims' routines and evaluate their security. You could be one of many people observed.

Follow these rules if you believe you are part of a pursuit

- The pursuit teams are not trained to attack the objectives, the can work moving or not; static surveillance will normally be carried out in the neighborhood, near your residence or office, trying to establish in and out hours. It is necessary to check the neighborhood for the presence of any suspicious people.

- Moving surveillance will be done pursuing the potential victim, trying to establish the routes used. If you suspect you are being persecuted, verify the fact, take an alternative route driving normally, discreetly, determine any information such as the make, color, license plate and the number and characteristics of the occupants.

- If the pursuit is confirmed, do not continue the trip, and reach the nearest security office. Never continue the trip heading for home if you are being pursued.

- Notify the adequate authority immediately, if you have a radio transmitter, call giving your exact position and place, the intentions and description of the pursuers.

- The people who are being pursued, should never stop or adopt any confrontation actions, but act as if nothing happens and do no let the pursuers know they have been uncovered.

IF ATTACKED

If you think the attack is imminent, for example, if the occupants of the car pursuing you take out their guns and weapons, drive to the nearest security office (never take the way home). If this is not possible, take immediate evasive actions as follows:

- Maneuver in all directions, if it is necessary to cross an intersection, a traffic jam, on a red light, drive against traffic, do it very carefully, if necessary to run on the sidewalk, at a maximum speed of 37 mph. and at angles of 30 and 45 degrees when turning. Avoid being stuck at all times; do not stop your vehicle.

- Increasing the distance between you and the pursuers by speeding up as an evasive tactic is functional only to gain time and be able to take another action to face the danger, it is important to know how maneuverable the car is as well as its limitations at high speeds.

- Do not lose control of the car at any time, and remember that an increase in the speed of the car means also an increase in the chances of a car accident.

- Stay alert so as not to get in between cars, trucks or motorcycles, when possible remain in the center of the road and have the space to maneuver.

- If you have a radio transmitter, ask for help and give your destination, intention, and identification of the attackers and of the vehicle, as well as indicate if there is anyone wounded.

If attacked with a napalm-like bomb, the windows may resist the impact if closed, the fuel will burn but in the exterior of the car, escape from the area at maximum speed, once away of it and save from a new attack, abandon the vehicle through the opposite side to the one in flames.

If attacked with a gun, you should try to stay below the window level and remain there. 9mm. and 30-mm. ammunition will normally penetrate the car's structure, however, the bullets can be deviated and their power is reduced significatively.

Any weapon attack must be repelled in order to escape under fire. The escape must be fast and heading to a police or military refuge.

In the eventual case of being near a firing line between terrorists and Special Forces, you should not move. Similar experiences have demonstrated that any moving thing is a target.

PROCEDURE FOR THE USE OF GUNS

When using guns for self-defense, keep in mind the following:

- No gun should be carried or manipulated when under the effects of alcohol or drugs.

- No gun should be carried or manipulated under the effects of medicine treatment affecting the reflexes of the person.

- No gun should be carried or manipulated six hours before the intake of alcohol.

- When carrying a gun, it should be covered at all times.

- A gun should not be taken out if it is not be used.

- A gun should not be used for personal defense when it is evident that the incident is a pocket or watch theft or a minor robbery.

- The gun should be carried in a place that allows a quick use and not a comfortable place.

- Any person carrying a gun should have good criterion. Remember that he or she is the only one responsible for a misuse of the gun.

- As a general rule, the gun should be taken out in public only if you have a justified motive, are prepared and must use it.

- A gun will be fired only as the last resource to neutralize a lethal threat against the person being protected or against you.

- The warning shots will be fired only when you hope to minimize the danger to third parties.

- Firing at people escaping is justified only if there is a reasonable cause to believe that they are a threat to the protected person or you, otherwise it is not at all justified.

- Similarly, firing at a moving vehicle with the mere idea of capturing it is not practical or justified, it is way too dangerous for third parties.

ARMORED VEHICLES

Protection of important people is nowadays completed in this modern society by the use of an armored vehicle that everyone in such conditions refers to as a "shield" but which could also be a "trap".

The protection required by a person will be greater as less conventional the attack is, and it is precisely terrorism and criminal gangs where there is no measurement of the forces since they kill by the back and kidnap by surprise.

An unnoticed armored vehicle, because of its exterior appearance so identical to other vehicles of its kind but unarmored, is the most qualified way to protect life in those moments of a greater risk: moving in the public way. Terrorism and kidnapping criminal gangs have chosen vehicles as an extremely vulnerable objective due to its thin original structure and the fragile glass in their windows, as well as its dependence of the more and more jammed traffic, with its mandatory stops at traffic lights and jams, adding to all this the confinement in its interior of the people incapable them of a direct response, remaining exposed to the driver's ability and good luck.

THE ARMOR

It is the technique of placing transparent or opaque materials of such density that in low quantities correspond acceptable weights, with milimetrical thickness which at the same time ought to be hard and malleable, to be placed between a firing arm and its victim.

According to the determination of the risk of each person, a level of armor is established, which in response to such conventional trouble can be grouped as follows:

> For 7.62 mm and less
> For 44 magnum and less
> For 357 magnum and less
> For 9/19 mm and less

To obtain the required armor, it is used:

For the armoring of the opaque parts: glass fiber and carbonate fiber with ballistic-nylon, vitrofetone, and other polyester resins combined with hardened plaques of ballistic steel mixed with aluminum of magnesium which primary objective is to deform the bullet and the distribution of the power impact.

For the armoring of the clear parts, glass of two basic types:

- Multi-laminated of crystals and interlayer of butiral of polivinile.

- Multi-laminated of glass united by butirals of polivinile and policarbonate plates.

The first of the two, even when it guarantees the best visual possibilities, it is inconvenient because of the weight it gains to protect against bigger calibers for the thickness required. The second overcomes these inconveniences.

ACCESSORIES

Bulletproof tires
- Armored battery
- Blanket anti-hand machine gun
- Electronic siren
- Reinforced bumpers
- Radio, mobile phone
- Electric shock of 20 to 50 milliamperes, at the door handles.

- Fire system
- Bulletproof blinds for the radiator
- Tear-gas and or smoke thrower
- Polarized windows

A good foresight is the armored vehicle, when facing the risks of gunfire attacks or explosives, kidnappings and assaults that may happen in the streets and roads. It is ideal for entrepreneurs, executives, diplomats and military men.

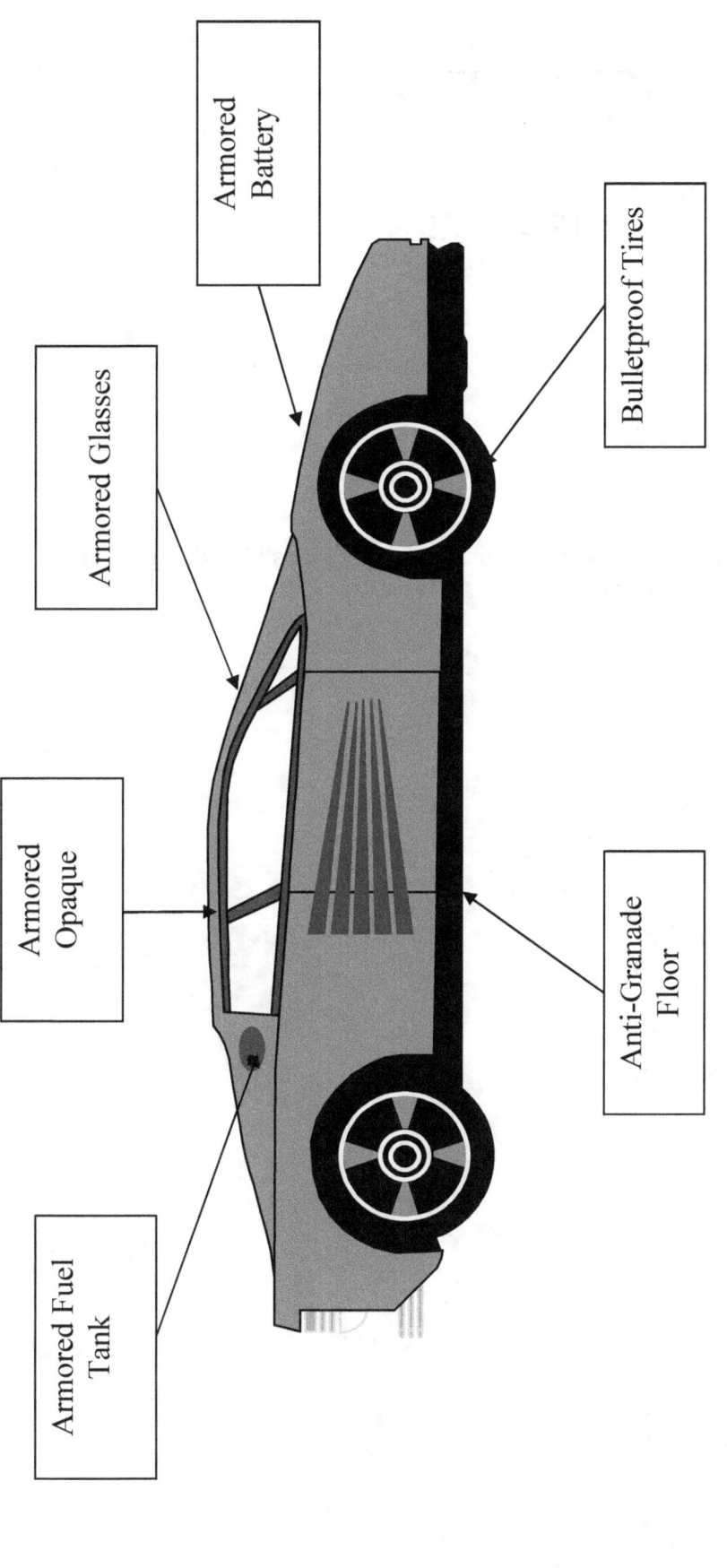

Armored Battery

Armored Glasses

Bulletproof Tires

Armored Opaque

Anti-Granade Floor

Armored Fuel Tank

CHAPTER IV

DISASTERS

DISATERS

Disasters are the group of grave damages of destructive proportions that affect the life, health, and goods of the community.

COMMON DISASTERS

Earthquakes, fires, torrential showers, floods, mudslides, landslides, droughts, epidemics, and blizzards are some of the common disasters.

KINDS OF DISASTERS

Natural:
- Earthquakes and tremors
- Tidal waves (tsunami)
- Landslides and mudslides
- Floods
- Alludes and rain storms
- Mudslides and overflowed rivers
- Electrical rainstorms
- Torrential showers
- Snowfalls and hailstorms
- Extreme temperatures
- Droughts
- Lightning
- Hurricanes and tornadoes
- Volcanic eruptions
- Hot and cold thermal tides
- Epidemics

Artificial
- Fires
- Explosions
- Massive transportation accidents
- Construction collapses
- Social commotion
- Wars

STATE OF EMERGENCY

A State of Emergency is the declaration of the Executive formulated by a Supreme Resolution as solicited by the National Civil Defense System, to attend proprietarily the effects of a disaster or calamity over a determined area to prevent the dangers of an imminent risk. It can be by sectors.

EARTHQUAKES

Earthquakes are deep vibrations of the earth's ground layers. Even today, there is not an established cause for such ground movements, but scientists state that they are the result of underground rock breaking affected by the geological phenomena of terrestrial mechanics, which have relation with the universal celestial laws.

Earthquakes happen between 10 and 600 kilometers of depth. When the intensity of such vibrations is low, it is called tremor, but when it is high, it is called earthquake.

SEISMIC SCALES

The Modified Mercalli Scale

One of the ways to determine the damage caused by the seismic movements is by using the seismic intensity scales. The best known and applied is the Modified Mercalli Scale, which consists of 12 degrees.

This scale gives us a qualitative measurement of the earthquake consequences. The scale has a disadvantage that its evaluation is affected by subjective factors, as to say, it is based on the sensations perceived by the observers during the earthquake.

INTENSITY SCALE

DEGREE	DESCRIPTION AND CONSEQUENCES
I.-	Perceived only by very sensitive instruments.
II.-	Perceived by some people resting, especially on high floors of buildings; some suspended objects swing.
III.-	It is detected in the interior of buildings but not always recognized as a tremor. It is possible to estimate the duration of the seism.
IV.-	Noticed inside houses and buildings by most people and outdoors by a few; parked vehicles swing noticeably.
V.-	Perceived by most people; at night some wake up; objects fall; pendulum clocks alter their rhythm.
VI.-	All persons perceive it; some panic and run outside, walking feel uneasy; there is detachment of finishing materials with minor damage.
VII.-	All people get scared, run outside and it is difficult to stay standing up. Drivers notice it.
VIII.-	It becomes difficult to drive any vehicle, walls and monuments collapse panels get loosen from their frames and porticoes.

IX.-	General panic; some buildings are displaced from their basements, collapses and ground cracks, dirt and mud comes out of the ground.
X.-	Almost total destruction of buildings, serious damage at major structures: bridges, damps and dikes; ground displacement.
XI.-	Railroads suffer big deformations, underground pipes break down.
XII.-	The damage is almost total; there are displacements of big rocks, objects jump into the air; perspectives get very distortioned.

The Ritcher Scale

The Ritcher Scale uses qualitative and quantitative media to establish the effects and the consequences of seismic movements. The quantitative evaluation is determined by measurement instruments, which relate the amount of energy freed during a seism. The Ritcher Scale has no top limits, it is improbable to have a seism of a bigger degree than nine because of the limitations of earth's crust.

PROCEDURES IN CASE OF A SEISM

Keep calm and safe

- Act with calmness and tell everybody else without despairing. Try to stay where you are since most accidents occur when trying to get in or out of unexpected places.

- A calm man thinks and acts better.

- Be aware that your nervousness may affect and cause greater damages than the disaster itself.

- Your frightened face and anxiety will scare others around you.

- If anyone gets desperate cries out or screams yell, "Slow down!" "Quiet!" so they will not lose control.

SPECIFIC ACTIONS

- If you are inside the first three floors of a building, take others orderly, without running, to the safe zone.

- If you are outside; move away and make sure others do so also, from electric wires, street lights or buildings that may collapse or cornices, flower pots, glass or adornments fall.

- If you are driving a vehicle, drive off the highway, stop immediately, get out of the car and watch the developing of the seism. Go under the car if objects are falling, when driving back; stay alert for those fallen objects you may find on the road or cracks.

- If you are at a wooden house, plan your evacuation at all times, do not hurry to go out, do it slowly, and avoid windows and porches.

- If you are at an old house, plan your evacuation at all times, get out of it quickly and orderly, stay away from porches and look for safe zones.

- If you are in a building, try to have people leave the building slowly and orderly to the safe zones; since the building will definitely shake due to the seism, do not hurry nor go down the swinging stairs or you might die if you fall down, do not use the elevator, stand below a beam, in a corner of the room or at a central column of the building staying away from windows.

- If it happens during work hours, do not use the elevator at all, workers should be calm so as to avoid running over others when going out; open the aisle and stair doors wide, control the way out of people to be ordered; be careful with the ones trapped in elevators, if this happens, try to get them out or call for and expertise help.

If It Happens at School

When students are inside, keep calm; teachers are in charge of the instructions to protect the children.

The teacher should teach the children about the nearest safe place from their position. This will help to avoid the danger in the long aisles and will get the best protection for them; if there would be any electrical devices functioning, turn them off.

Try not to let children leave the building running, it is a great danger. Have them get protection from beams, at doorframes, under desks, a table or any resistant piece of furniture capable of stand falling objects.

When students are outside, move them away from all dangerous structures; the distance that means security from a building is:

15 m. (20 steps) for single floor buildings.
25 m. (40 steps) for two-story buildings.
35 m. (60 steps) for three-story buildings

And so on.

Keep the students away from all hanging wires and keep them from running in the street near buildings or even entering them. Be careful with rubbish that falls in the street outside the buildings, especially next to the walls of the house.

EVACUATING AND ESCAPE ROUTES IN CASE OF SEISMS

Escape routes are the safest ways, signaled to evacuate a determined place in case of an emergency.

- The entire escape route should be kept clear.

- Check all the doors of the house, preferably the escape routes.

- Leave a duplicate of the key in the lock from the inside, in case it gets locked. You could need such door to escape, if you do not find the key quickly, you could provoke panic and desperation.

- If along the escape route there are stairs, these should have a handrail on both sides. You could roll down the stairs with no control and get badly hurt.

- Do not allow children to play neither at stairs nor neither doors nor they should leave their toys in the way. If your children are used to playing with little toys, teach them to put them away once they have finished playing with them. If they leave them near the stairs, doors or along the way, they could slip. SLIPPING MAY BE FATAL AND CAUSE WOUNDED PEOPLE AND PANIC.

- Eliminate those carpets, rugs loosen over lustrous floors. Never allow those on the first and last steps of the stairs. IT HAS BEEN PROVEN THAT SLIPPING OVER THEM HAS CAUSED FALLS DEALING WITH DEATHS. BE CAREFUL!

- THERE IS NO GOLDEN RULE TO ELIMINATE ALL THE DANGERS OF A SEISM, BUT MATERIAL ONES AND PERSONAL ACCIDENTS MAY BE CONSIDERABLY REDUCED IF PEOPLE FOLLOW PROTECTION RULES.

PREVENTION AND FIRE CONTROL

Fire

Fire is the result of a chemical reaction known as combustion, produced when three elements get in contact:

- A fueling material
- Heat
- Air

BASIC PROCEDURES TO FIGHT FIRE

- Cooling (elimination of heat)
- Suffocation (elimination of air)
- Removal (withdrawing of the material)

FIRE

It called fire the total or partial burning of a great quantity of fuel.

TYPES OF FIRE

Since not all fires can be put out the same way, it has been necessary to classify them according to some characteristics.

- **Class "A".** These are the fires produced in solid, common and dried materials. For example, the fires originated in paper, cardboard paper, fabrics, synthetic fibers and wood, trash, plastic, rubber, etc., a characteristic of it is that fire penetrates the fuel, it necessary to have a penetrating extinguisher to put out the reaction. The best way to fight it is with **water**.

- **Class "B".** These are the fires produced over flammable liquids for example in: gasoline, alcohol, benzene, ether, hexane, on fueling liquids such as oil, kerosene, paint; on fueling gases such as propane, acetylene, hydrogen. A characteristic of it is that vapor and gases burn and the separation of the liquid producing the gases are required. Unlike class "A" fires these are superficial. Eliminating the fuel, by suffocation or cooling may put out all these fires.

- **Class "C".** These are fires produced by electricity (short circuits) at supplies and electrical equipment. They must be put out after shutting down the electrical service or using extinguishers of dry chemical powder or carbonic gas.

- **Class "D".** These fires are produced because of the metals and fuels, for example: Mg, K, Al, Zn, Na, Ti, and Zr. To put these it necessary to use special extinguishers.

SECURITY PROCEDURE IN CASE OF FIRES

DURING THE FIRE

General Actions

Plan on locating the exit and keep calm. Do not face an unproportional fire; make sure everybody leaves before and try to call the fire department. If the fire has just begun, contain all the flammable materials and try to control it. Once the fire starts, tell those who live with you and begin work. If there is fire and an extinguisher and you know how to use it, **use it!**

Special Actions

If you are trapped in a fire and you are in a two-story building or house, do not jump and wait for help. If you can get out of the place do it, but do not allow anyone to get back to it. If you are trapped in a fire and you cannot use the exits close the door and seal the borders to keep the smoke out, it is preferable to get shelter in a room with windows to the street or outside. The windows should be wide open to increase ventilation. It is recommended to throw anything through those windows to help you call for assistance.

If a Person Gets Caught in the Smoke

Try to be the closest to the floor because there the air is the least contaminated. Your respirations must be short, through the nose, with a handkerchief or something similar (if it is possible to wet it) and crawl for the exit.

If You Try to Escape from the Fire

Touch the door before opening it. If it is hot or the smoke is getting through it, **DO NOT OPEN IT!** Look for another exit. If the doors are cool, open them carefully.

If Someone's Clothes Catch on Fire

Order the person to lie on the floor covering up face and neck. Make him or her roll down on the floor, and then cover the person with a blanket to put the fire out.

If the fire is during work hours

If there is a fire alarm pull it, shut off the electricity, try to put out the fire with the appropriate ways for that (fire extinguishers, fire hoses, axes, etc.), open all exterior windows, watch out for the personnel to leave orderly and calmly; call the fire-fighters and ambulances, using the direct lines at hand.

FIRE EXTINGUISHER AGENTS

The main and most common are:

Water. It can be used as water vapor, fog or blasts. Water fog is easy to obtain using special water pipes. Water blasts should only be used when it is required to reach long distances or perform a penetrating action through the fueling materials. It is vital to remember that to use water, we should shut the electricity off in the area.

Foam. Chemical foams are formed when aluminium sulphate reacts with sodium bicarbonate in the presence of water.

Dry chemical dust. There exist dry chemical dusts having different features each of them, not being electric conducting, texture, density, speed of exit, etc.

- Sodium or potassium bicarbonate based: when applied over fire they produce carbonic gas and water steam, it has suffocating effects.

- Ammonium monophosphate based; is used to put out the three types of fire. It has better qualities than bicarbonates.

- Potassium Chloride based or sulphate, these are known as "k purpure" or "Super K" and present greater extensive power over the three types of fire.

Inert gases. These extinguisher agents put out fires by suffocation, among the best known are carbon dioxide (CO_2) and antioxygen (N^2) that are heavier than air and thus they displace it. They do not conduct electricity, which makes them excellent to put out class "C" fires. In addition, there exist other gases such Halon that chemically blocks the molecular reaction of fire.

FIRE PREVENTION

Fire prevention consists on avoiding the three elements (fuelling material-heat-oxygen) to get combined.

PREVENTITIVE ACTIONS

- Instruction programs

- Get equipment to fight fires

- Form teams of firefighters

- Get portable fire extinguishers

- Give preference to BC dry chemical powder extinguishers.

- Appoint someone responsible for the maintenance of the extinguishers and automatic systems.

If the Fire is on a Different Floor

Once the alarm is heard, verify where the fire comes from; check for open doors and windows unroll fire hoses; be ready to shut the electricity off if the fire is close; do not move people, until the real magnitude of the fire is known; in such cases, do not use elevators but stairs only.

If There Are People Trapped in an Elevator

First take people out and then start the emergency lights system.

If the Fire Happens During Non-work Hours

People in charge of the building at that time should follow the same procedures: shut off the electricity (except for the water pump), call the firemen; put the emergency lights to work; if there are any people trapped in elevators, set them free; call the people responsible for the office.

During a Special Event

Using loudspeakers, try to keep the people calm. Let them know that all security aspects have been taken care of to keep the situation under control and at the same time, tell them to exit in order. If necessary, call the fire department, use fire extinguishers and use the sand from the buckets, ask the police for back up. Call emergency department at the hospital. Continually remind the people to keep calm until their evacuation is total.

Fire Rescue

When trying to help a person, whose clothes are burning, do the following:

- Wrap the person in a coat, a bed sheet or rug leaving the head uncovered.

- Try to put out the fire around the head and shoulders and downwards to the feet.

- If you do not have anything at hand, make the person turn slowly on the floor and put out the flames with your hands.

- If the person tries to run away, they should be stopped and push down to the floor. It is necessary to have the person on the floor since you are trying to stop the fire. If they run, their clothes will burn faster, in they sit or stand up, and they can be killed immediately by inhaling flames or hot air.

Precautions

Hot air or flame inhalations can kill the one who is helping. Do not face the flames directly. It is effective to turn aside and avoid direct contact with the flames to not inhale gases.

If you try to escape from a floor or building in flames you have to be careful of opening doors, corridors or stairs. If there is a fire in a building, there is usually accumulation of hot air in corridors and stairways.

It is necessary to open doors carefully to feel the temperature in the corridors and hallways. If it feels very hot, do not open, especially if there are other exits.

It is to be understood that open windows and doors will create a flow of air and will quicken the fire so they should not be opened unless you are ready to go out.

If you face the problem of helping a wounded person from a high floor, you can improvise a rope made of tied bed sheets, curtains, or other materials. (Make simple double knots). One end of the rope will be tied to a heavy or solid object inside the building and the other end around the wounded person's arms. If the person can be descended safely, this rope will be used later. It is necessary to recommend the people trapped in a building in flames not to jump out the high floors except as a last resource.

It has been said that the "breathable" air in a burning space is by the floor, but this is only partially true. There are less flames and smog in the low zones of the atmosphere, near the floor air can be cooler, however, near the floor as well as near the ceiling, there can be carbon monoxide and other lethal gases. If possible use an oxygen mask or other breathing devices to penetrate a space in flames. If you do no have those, cover your mouth and nose with wet linen to diminish the risk of inhaling hot air or smoke. This does not protect from toxic gases or lack of oxygen.

FLOODS

Floods are the slow or quick invasion of rivers, lakes, and ponds over populated areas. They overflow when the volumes of the riverbed brim over the normal.

Rainy seasons generally result in obstruction of roads and railroads, as consequence of mudslides and floods because of overflowing rivers, streams and irrigation canals; all of which make difficult the transit of vehicles from supplying centers to markets and vice versa, which generates a shortage of fuel, groceries and products for the normal development of cities.

DAMAGES PRODUCED

Floods can destroy populated areas built on cement and bricks, adobe, quincha, tapial, etc., by wetting the basements and walls, provoking their collapse.

- It can create grave problems of water supply and drainage

- Because of a lack in the supply of drinking water and the impossibility of evacuating black waters, which together with heat, provoke epidemics and parasites by multiplying the insects, which carry those diseases.

- Floods also damage crops due to the excess of water.

- Paradoxically, the fire is a danger closely related to floods. The grow of waters can push down oil or gasoline tanks or invade fuel storages and spill their content in vast areas; if those fuels burn, fire will spread quickly enough since floating object give abundant fuelling material. Short circuits in the electric systems of buildings can provoke fires and electrocutions.

ACTIONS TO TAKE

If a Flood Is Announced

- Store additional water in clean containers. Water supply can be interrupted.

- If it is necessary to leave your home, and there is plenty of time to take the essentials with you to a safe place, DO IT!

- You must evacuate immediately, without desperation and before the crossing is interrupted by the water.

If You Have a Vehicle

Keep it with fuel since at an emergency gas stations may run short on supply.

IF A PERSON IS DROWNING

If the One Drowning is by the Shore

- Hand him/her a shirt, stick or a branch.

- Bring him out to shore

If You Have a Lifeguard Ring

- Tie a rope to the lifeguard ring.

- Throw it to the water. Pull it by the rope, once the victim has reached it, so they can be safe.

If You Can Swim and the Victim is Far From Shore

- Go in the water until it is at chest level.

- Stand firmly.

- Grab the victim by his/her wrist

- Pull slowly.

If You Cannot Swim and the Victim is Far From Shore

- Throw the victim a towel, an inner tube or any other object that can help the victim to stay afloat.

- Get help to bring the victim safe to shore.

DURING A FLOOD

- Keep yourself in a secure area.

- Do not cross by the flooded areas since you are not aware of their depth.

- Do not eat any fresh foods that have been in contact with the water.

- Do not stay in the disaster area unless your presence is necessary

- Do not manipulate any electrical equipment that is turned on within the affected zones. The electrical equipment must be checked and dried before it is used again.

- Use lanterns, but candlelight's to examine things, there can be flammable substances inside.

AFTER A FLOOD

- Tune up a radio station during the emergency.

- Avoid crossing by flooded zones. Erosion may have occurred on the floor and you could get scratched or cut.

- It is necessary to get vaccinated.

- Check for the stability of you house before you start drying it out because it may collapse.

- Proceed to dry your house burning firewood or the like doors closed in the middle of the rooms and ventilating from time to time.

- Take out and get rid of decomposed foods, dead animals, etc.

- Boil the water before using it.

- Inform authorities about disabled public line services.

www.ingramcontent.com/pod-product-compliance
Lightning Source LLC
Chambersburg PA
CBHW081248180526
45170CB00007B/2347